Drives Away

Victoria Ray

BookLeaf Publishing

Presentation by *BookLeaf Publishing*

Web: www.bookleafpub.com

E-mail: info@bookleafpub.com

ISBN: 9789357614528

First edition 2022

I dedicate this to my parents and to Lisa.

Good Grief

Loneliness becomes her?
I lie in wait, waiting, waiting.
My family left.
Shades on, and shades down
Sea goes on and on
Back to reality,
Back to autopilot.
Watch as my happiness ascends on a plane.
My family left.

Joyride

The joy of seeing your car turn the corner
It's been both a long time and nothing at all
When you smile in my direction, I cannot
breathe
The joy of taking your hand in mine
Not letting go, never letting go
Convincing myself this is real
Keeping the demon from you
Trying to stop him from fucking it up
Failing.
The joy of once having had you in my arms
Does not make it better.
My happiness drove away.

Longing

Am I allowed? Should I? Should I?
Been five minutes, ten minutes, a day
I'll get her into trouble.
Don't then.
I must.
I miss her.
She'll get into trouble
and then where'll you be?
It's hard.
I know.
What do I do?
Tell me what to do.
You wait.
I can't--
You can.
It's hard.
I know.

Mind Preoccupied

Keeping straight faces
Ears prick up
Absorbent thoughts
Absences of concentration
Slow time, slow time, fast time
Slow time.
Smelling memories, involuntary smiles
Touches, whispers, glances, pictures
Slow time, slow time, fast time
Slow time.
Voluntary smiles.

Renew

Hey you, hey you, hey you.
It's true, it's true, it's true.
It's been far, it's been far too long
To sing this song with you.

Hey you, hey you, hey you,
I'm blue, I'm blue, I'm blue.
I've been waiting so damn long
To sing this song for you.

Hey you, hey you, hey you.
It's true, it's true, it's true.
Have you been waiting long?
I know I've been gone so long,

Hey you, hey you, hey you,
I knew, I knew, I knew
You wouldn't wait for me,
I was tired of not being free.

Hey you, hey you, hey you.
I rue, I rue, I rue
Not calling up on you,
I heard? You're doing it anew.

Hey you, hey you, hey you,
It's untrue, not true, it's true.
No, never saw that girl before.
What did you come here for?

Hey you, hey you, hey you,
We're through, we're through, we're through
No more tears, no tears for you
Don't want nothing from you.

Hey you, hey you, hey you,
This is new, it's new, we're new.
I want to know more about You
Let's go someplace New.

Fresh Air

A draught of air rolls in through an open door,
I hear a door further away slam shut in return.
Draughts make me uncomfortable,
Whatever I'm doing, there's the thought in the
back of my mind telling me there's a draught
The thought gets bigger and bigger, and I try to
ignore it
Until it fills my mind, distracts
And I put up the white flag
And I get up to close the door
And then I'm comfortable again.

You are that draught.

Drawing Her In

You are oxygen.
I breathe you in.
Inhale your scent.

You are hope.
I want you in.
Inhale your presence.

You are love.
I let you in.
Exhale my past,
inhale your present.

You are mine.

Haphazard

Worried, foreboding
Why am I so anxious?
Something's happened
Turn on the TV
No, don't!
But something's happened
I can't watch
I can
I can't watch
I must.
Those poor people
Something's happened.

Transference

Does it end? This existence
which has me doubled over in pain
Love, she's arrived
Loaded with bags of care and attention
Anticipating, soothing, there.
Her affection moves me
But I can't move
Her feeling touches me
But I can't touch her
Salt drips quietly down my face
Able to transfer pain for a time
I sleep, relaxed while she is there.

Paralysed

He's sitting there, I sense it
Keep your eyes shut, it's just a dream
He's staring there, I know it
Keep your mouth shut, it's just a dream
He's waiting there, so be it
Keep your legs shut, it's just a dream.
Try to break free, tap your little finger
Don't let him see, try to breathe harder

She nudges you awake.
He's not there. It was just a dream.

Whole Number

When I see you, I am whole again.
When I smell you, I am myself again.
When I touch you, I am together again.
You're it.

Forget-Me-Not

Calendar stuck a knife in me again.
What day of May is it this time?
I decide to flip the calendar of my mind like a rolodex…
Fifteen years, has it been?
Don't think about it, don't, don't
Shake your memories away, let the toxic nonsense disintegrate
Allow the fear and despair to dissipate
Won't think about it, won't, won't
Will.

Helplessness

How to help her?
Silence.
She's crying?
In silence.
What do you need?
To be in silence.
What can I do?
Leave me to be in silence.
Goodbye then.

Please.
Don't leave me to be in silence.

Suffice to Say

In my dreams, I am inadequate.
Days of autopilot
My body is waiting for something
That my mind is not aware of yet.
Life is a journey, they say
Yet it is filled with nonsensical medals
When is enough, enough?
Even in my dreams, I am inadequate.

Psychological Warfare

Anemones. One word I can never say.
Anemones. Word loses all meaning.
Anema, nema, nemones.
Making them uncomfortable,
Embarrassed looks, no, pitying
Blood rushes up
Anemones. Anemones. Lost track.
Water for the anemones.
Three warriors in my head
Intelligence versus intuition versus instinct
Who will win?
Not the anemones.

Synapses Collapsing

Devastating. Four syllables
I roll inside my head
De - va - state - ing

Recall is not as good as it once was
Blended aroma of hickory smoke and glasses of
milk
Scraped knees and tags of you're it!

Difficulty remembering,
Neurons receiving a poor signal
Specialist after specialist
Bench outside, hiding
Cannot face the login
Unavailability not an option
Please. Let me be.

Miasma. Three syllables.
Me-as-ma.
No, that would never work
No patience.
Is grass greener? I wonder

Deliberation. Weighing up

Chemistry

Under the weather, that's what they say
Isn't it? The typical excuse
Cramp in the legs, shooting pains in the head
Insincere affectation or a few screws loose?
Appointments are made, but every time I spill my guts
I'm treated as if I'm uttering untruths.
Until the one that listens. Or rather hears,
Hears what I have to say.
After so many days, months, years.
Almost as good as pain relief.
Almost.

The One

Why is she here? Why? Why?
Why does she stay?
I can't believe that I'm her one.
Is it a lie?

Our souls resonate, I've never felt hate
From her.
There is no stagnation of our love toward one another.
Day breaks, then night.
Our eyes awake, and see light.

Pushing and pulling, I try.
But my love, she only guides.
Am I her one? Why? Why?
She is my one. That is no lie.

Or So I Thought

You are nothing I ever wanted.
Or so I thought.
Neither the chaser or the chased.
We are equal.

Churning, my stomach dropped when I used to look at you
And you turned around
Not focused on me but I kept yearning
That one day you'd finally see
Me, and discern that I
Cared for you
Thought of nothing but you
Could not control my movements around you.

Puzzling, you stayed despite the games
And ups and downs and calling of names
Chiselling at my different cold layers
And plays and lack of faith.
Learning the lines of your face, the shadows in your eyes
The need in your skin, the possibilities in your mind
Hurting you was not possible.
Losing you was.

You were everything I never wanted.
I was in awe. So I fought.
Yet you overtook me and I overtook you.
We are equal.
Now I have Everything.

The Day Before Yesterday

Quiet. Placid.
Looking at old birthday cards.
Studying the pen strokes, echoing them with my fingers
Realising these old names had loved me.

Calm. Slower.
Looking at old photographs.
Recalling fragments long since forgotten about
Balancing nostalgia with slight waves of wretchedness.

Sad. Serene.
Looking at old certificates.
Travelling back to the time where the priority was validation
Timing when the alarm clock faded away.

Awe. Wonder.
Looking at new wedding rings.
Remembering the happiness of the day before yesterday
Smiling at the person sleeping next to me.

My Happiness Drives Away

How refreshing true love is.
Not having to struggle to fit in
Not having to compromise about every little thing
Not having to act.

How enjoyable true love is.
Being who one wants to be
Being able to like whatever I want
Without judgment and criticism.

How enlightening true love is.
Never knowing there was a person out there
Who actually loves you, truly loves you
And sets no condition, even on your condition.

How confident true love is.
Having absolute faith and trust in one person
That you don't even think about them being faithful and trustworthy
You just know.

How lovely true love is.
Knowing that when your happiness drives away
They will be back in time for dinner.

Printed in the USA
CPSIA information can be obtained
at www.ICGtesting.com
LVHW020611030124
767932LV00004B/313

9 789357 614528